The Baby

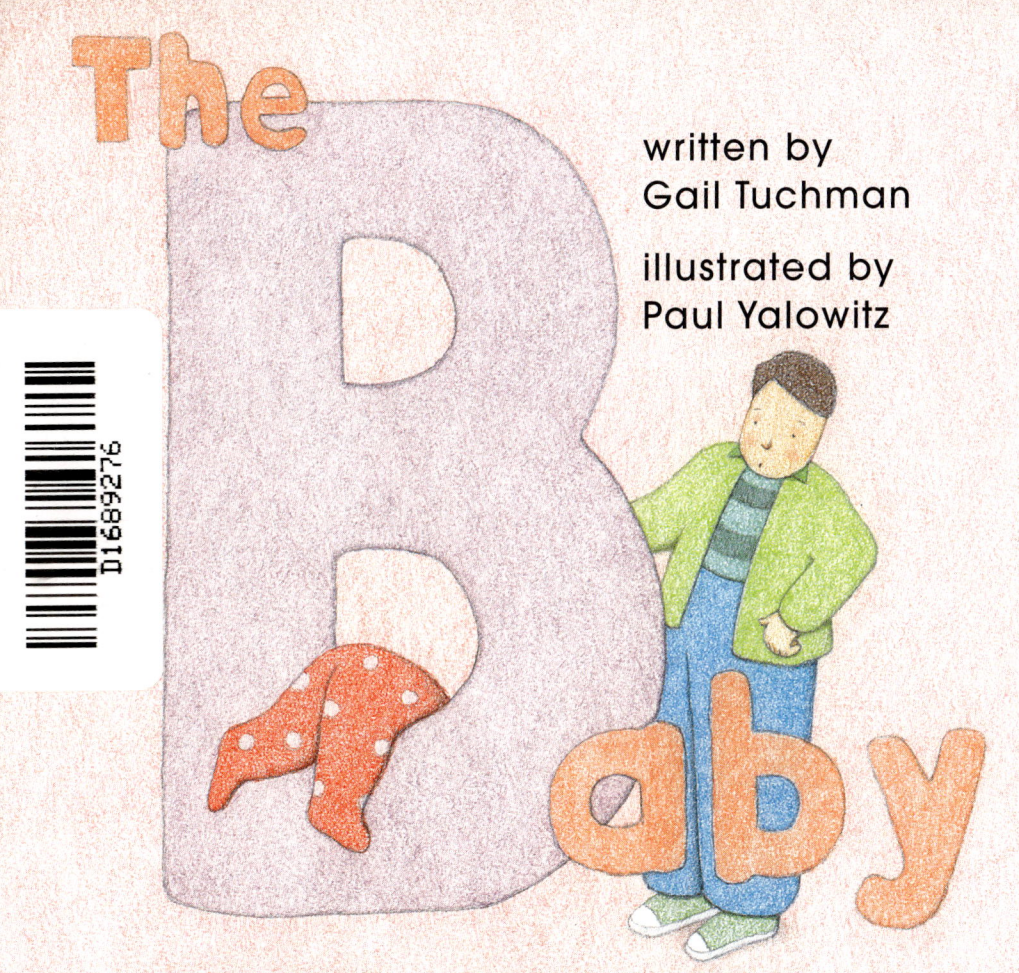

written by
Gail Tuchman

illustrated by
Paul Yalowitz

HARCOURT BRACE & COMPANY

Orlando Atlanta Austin Boston San Francisco Chicago Dallas New York
Toronto London

The baby has my block.

The baby has my lock.

The baby has my rock.

The baby has my clock.

The baby has my sock.

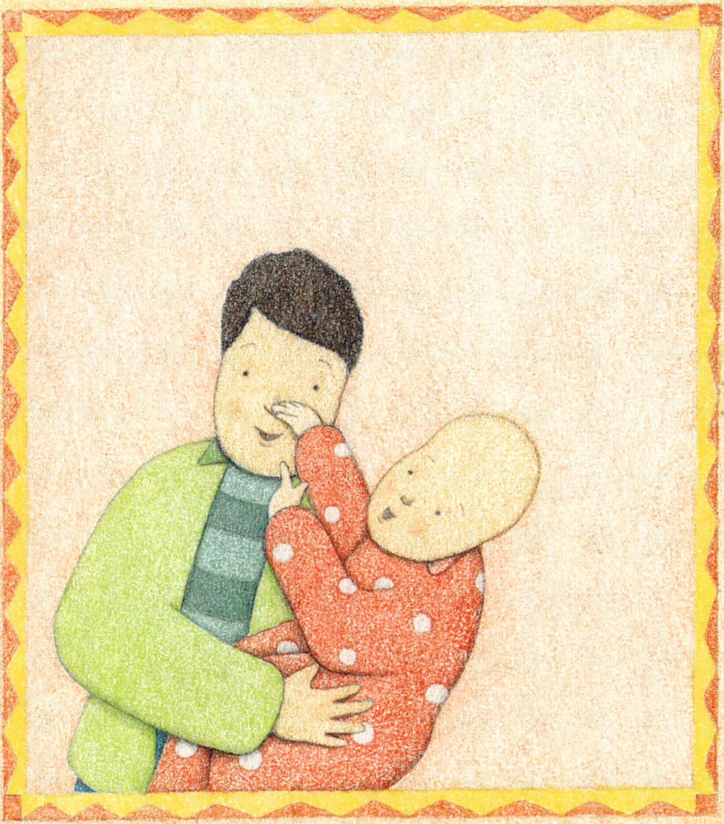

The baby has me!